# Charlotte Brontë

Written by Harriet Castor
Illustrated by Ismael Pinteño

## Contents

| | |
|---|---|
| Famous author | 2 |
| Beginnings | 4 |
| Off to school | 12 |
| Inspiration | 16 |
| Becoming a teacher | 24 |
| Brussels | 34 |
| A chance discovery | 38 |
| Publication | 48 |
| Sorrowful times | 58 |
| A taste of fame | 64 |
| Changes at home | 70 |
| Legacy | 74 |
| Glossary | 76 |
| Index | 77 |
| The Brontës' world | 78 |

**Collins**

# Famous author

In early 19th century England, life for women was very unfair. Women were believed to be **inferior** to men. They couldn't vote, or go to college or university, and they were only allowed to have a few types of job. Women were expected to obey the men in their families, and after marriage they didn't even exist, in law, as separate people. The law viewed a husband and wife as one person – and that person was the man. If a married woman worked, her wages belonged to her husband. She couldn't own anything, even if it had belonged to her before the marriage. She couldn't divorce her husband, and she had no rights over her children.

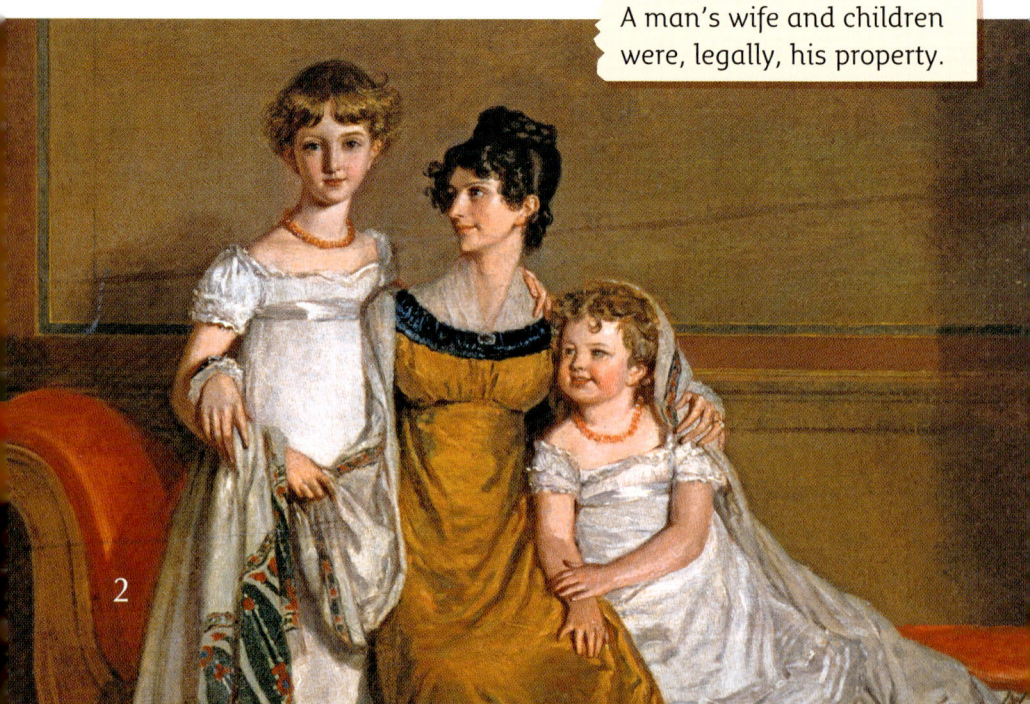

A man's wife and children were, legally, his property.

Given this, it's not surprising that female authors were extremely rare. To write a book, you need to think for yourself – and have something to say. Since women were supposed to obey men, they weren't expected to have opinions of their own. When women did write, their books were judged unfairly, just because they hadn't been written by men. Despite this, a girl grew up in England at this time who was determined to be a writer. She knew her work was just as good as any man's. What's more, her stories were brave and **pioneering**. She created heroines who were independent and intelligent, who had strong opinions and who cared more for truth than social rules. This shocked some people, but it **inspired** many others – her books became bestsellers. The writer's name was Charlotte Brontë. This is her story.

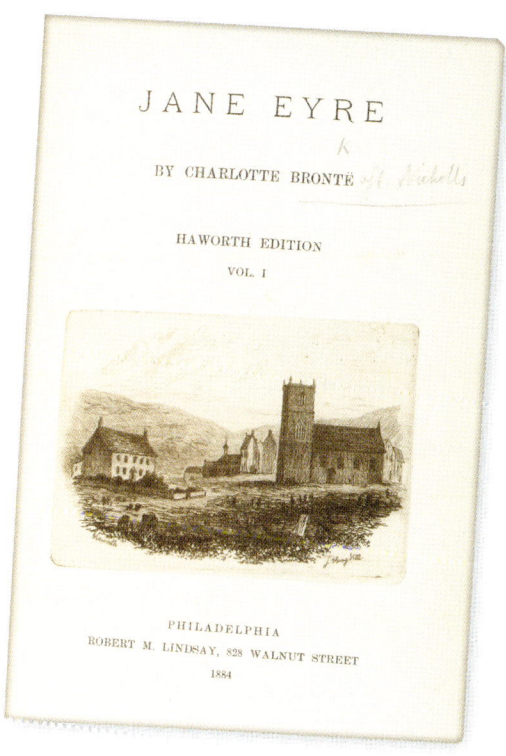

# Beginnings

Charlotte was born on 21 April 1816 in Yorkshire, in the north of England. Her father, Patrick, was a **clergyman**. The family lived in a **parsonage** in the village of Thornton.

Little Charlotte already had two older sisters, and soon more siblings arrived. First there was a brother. He was named Branwell, because their mother's surname had been Branwell before her marriage. Soon afterwards, two more sisters were born: Emily and Anne.

The month Charlotte turned four, the family moved to another Yorkshire village, called Haworth. Haworth was built on the side of a hill, and was surrounded by wild **moorlands**. It was a place of strong winds and bleak beauty. The Brontës' new home was Haworth parsonage. It was on the edge of the village, at the top of a very steep street, with views over the moors beyond.

The Brontë children grew to love these moors, and the Haworth parsonage was to be Charlotte's home for the rest of her life.

the parsonage at Haworth

Haworth was a small but busy place, with shops, warehouses and inns. Many of the villagers worked in the textile mills and sandstone quarries nearby. But health in Haworth was poor, because the water supply and drainage systems were very old. There were no sewers at all, and waste ran in open gutters down the streets. Many people died young in Haworth, and the churchyard next to the parsonage was very full.

Today, Haworth is a popular destination for tourists.

When Charlotte was only five, her mother – Maria – died. It was a desperately sad time for the whole family. During Maria's illness, her sister – Aunt Branwell – had come to help with the children. Now Aunt Branwell agreed to stay to look after them. Charlotte's father was very busy with his duties in the **parish**. In any case, looking after children wasn't seen as a fit job for a man.

Aunt Branwell

Aunt Branwell was a lively, independent woman who wasn't afraid of expressing her views, even when she disagreed with Patrick. She came from Cornwall – a warmer part of England – and she didn't like the cold weather in Yorkshire. However, she had a strong sense of duty, and this was what made her stay.

A typical day for Charlotte and her brother and sisters began with prayers in their father's study. Then, after a breakfast of porridge and bread, their father taught them school lessons. Next, Charlotte and her sisters practised their sewing with Aunt Branwell. For dinner they often ate roast meat, with rice pudding for dessert. Afternoons were spent walking on the moors, and this was the children's favourite part of the day. They had great fun running about and playing games.

The eldest child, who was called Maria after their mother, often read to the others from newspapers. They invented games based on stories in the news, or on tales their father had told them from history. Charlotte's favourite character was the Duke of Wellington, who'd won a great victory over the French leader Napoleon Bonaparte at Waterloo the year before Charlotte was born.

Sometimes, the servants took part in the children's games. Sarah, the cook, once played the part of a prince, with a bedcover for her cloak. The prince had to escape, so Sarah climbed out of a window on to a tree branch. The branch broke. Sarah was unhurt, but the children got into trouble with their father!

Patrick Brontë was an **eccentric** man. He slept with a loaded pistol by his bed, and every morning he'd empty it by firing a shot from the bedroom window. This surprised guests who stayed at the parsonage! He cared very much for the poor in his parish, and campaigned to make life better for them. Patrick came from a poor family himself. He'd been born in Ireland, and had worked hard at school and then won a place at university in England.

Patrick Brontë

Now that he was a clergyman, he was considered a "gentleman", but he didn't have much money. When his children grew up, they'd have to work for their living. There were choices of jobs for boys, but very few jobs were thought suitable for the daughters of a gentleman. The best option was to be a teacher. For this, Charlotte and her sisters needed a good education.

Patrick realised he couldn't teach all six children himself at home, so he decided to send his older girls to school. The school he chose was at Cowan Bridge in Lancashire. Maria and Elizabeth, the oldest Brontë sisters, went there first. A few months later, Charlotte and Emily joined them.

Cowan Bridge school

# Off to school

Charlotte was eight when she went to Cowan Bridge. It was a boarding school, and she was miserable there. This wasn't only because she was homesick – it was also because the pupils at Cowan Bridge were very badly treated. There wasn't enough food, and Charlotte suffered terrible pains from hunger. The meals she did get were prepared badly in a filthy kitchen, and often weren't fit to be eaten. The teachers were harsh and punished the girls cruelly, often by beating them.

Here's an example of a Victorian school.

Many girls at Cowan Bridge fell ill and died. Two of them were Charlotte's older sisters, Maria and Elizabeth. Maria was treated harshly by one teacher, even when she was seriously ill. Charlotte never forgot Maria's bravery, and later based a character on Maria in one of her most famous books.

## *Tuberculosis*

Maria and Elizabeth Brontë died of tuberculosis – an infectious disease that usually attacks the lungs. People who live in poor, overcrowded conditions and don't have enough food – like the girls at Cowan Bridge – have a higher risk of catching it. Today, tuberculosis can be treated, and prevented with vaccines. In Charlotte Brontë's time, there were no medicines to fight it.

After their sisters' deaths, Charlotte and her younger sister Emily were brought back to live at home. Charlotte was now the eldest child. She felt responsible for looking after the others – Branwell, Emily and Anne – even though she was only nine.

The children had lessons with their father and Aunt Branwell. They studied the Bible every day, and often walked to a nearby town to borrow books from a library. They loved to read tales from the *Arabian Nights* and *Aesop's Fables*, and to practise their drawing by copying illustrations. They also loved a magazine called *Blackwood's*, which included book reviews, political news and lots of funny pieces about the famous people of the day.

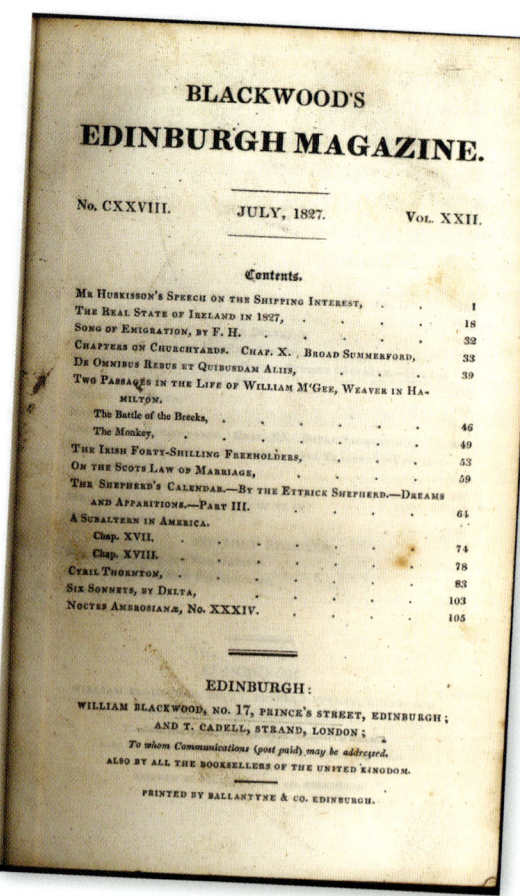

The Brontë children loved playing with toy soldiers.

The Brontës had toys too, including alphabet blocks, skittles and dolls. One day, when Charlotte was ten, her father bought Branwell some new toy soldiers. Each of the children chose one as their special friend. Charlotte called hers Wellington, Branwell's was called Bonaparte, Emily called hers Gravey (because his face looked serious, or "grave") and Anne named her soldier Waiting Boy.

# Inspiration

Branwell's new set of soldiers became known as the "Twelves" or the "Young Men". As they played with them, the Brontës made up stories, inspired by their favourite books and magazines, and by the adventures of famous explorers whom they read about in the newspapers. Sometimes the children featured in the stories themselves, as huge, monster-like **genii** called Tallii (Charlotte), Brannii (Branwell), Emmii (Emily) and Annii (Anne).

This miniature book was handwritten by Charlotte when she was 14.

Inspired by their father's geography books, Charlotte and her siblings set their stories in made-up lands that were part of their own imaginary version of Africa. Sometimes there were battles in these lands, and they'd act out the battles with the soldiers, in the parsonage garden or on the moors. This was great fun, and the soldiers got very battered.

Soon, the children began writing down the stories and games, and making them into tiny home-made books. Even though the writing inside the books was extremely small, they made it look like print, as if the books had been published.

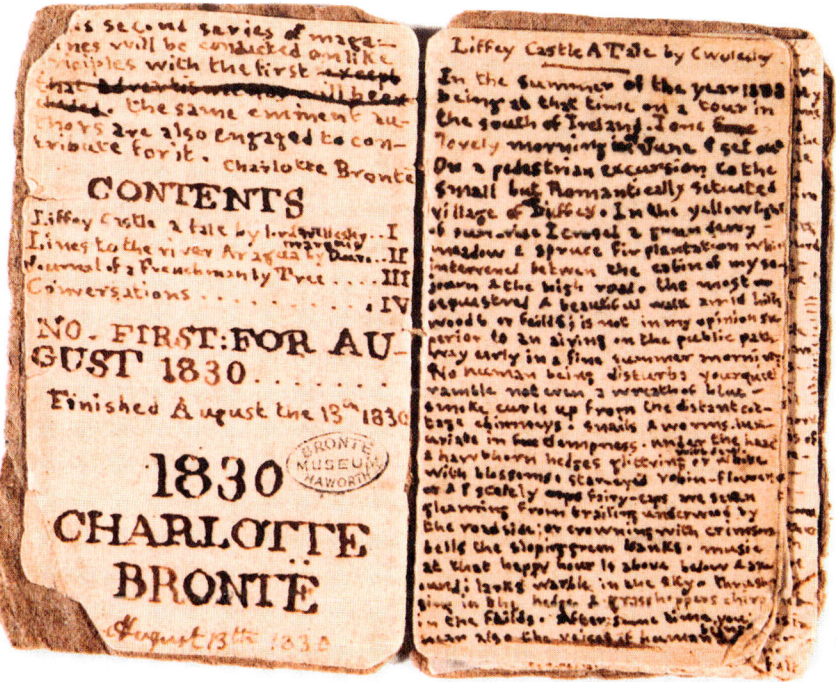

Charlotte and her siblings began to spend more and more time writing. They loved it so much that they joked about having "scribblemania", and they dreamt of being published authors one day. As their stories became more detailed and complicated, they worked in two pairs: Charlotte and Branwell wrote about a place called Angria, while Emily and Anne made up a place called Gondal.

Charlotte and Branwell competed against each other with their writing, and sometimes their characters had great arguments. They wrote poems, letters, histories and little novels for and about the Twelves. They even invented a language for them, and produced a monthly magazine, inspired by *Blackwood's*, which Charlotte called *The Young Men's Magazine*.

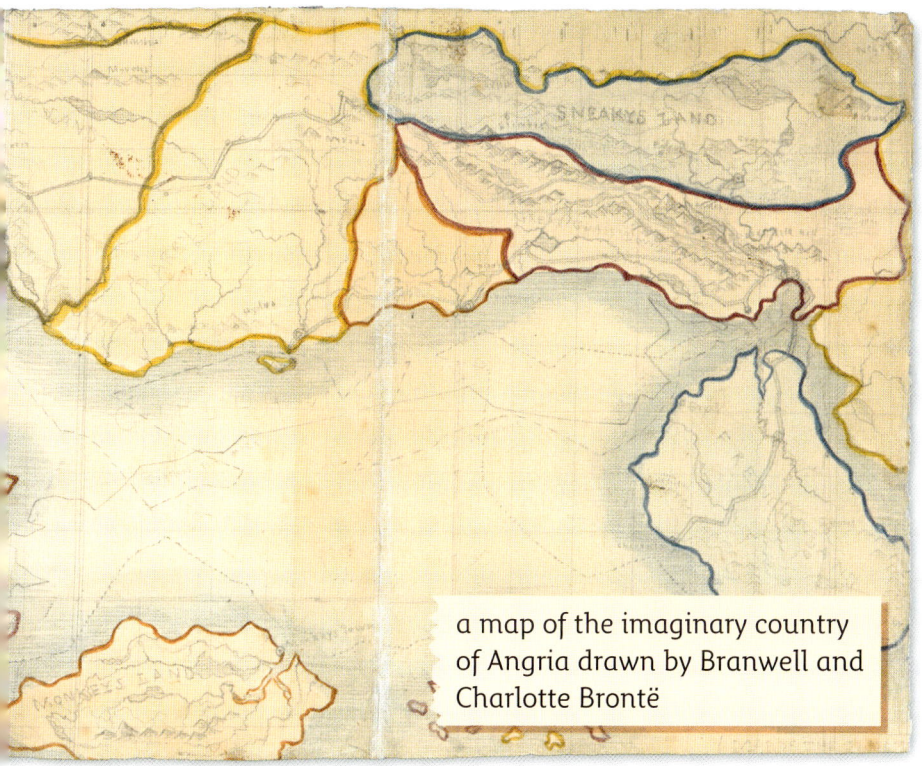

a map of the imaginary country of Angria drawn by Branwell and Charlotte Brontë

The books and magazines were too tiny for their father and aunt to read, so their imaginary world was a wonderful secret.

Charlotte would have loved to carry on writing and playing at home. However, her father was still worried about preparing his children for work. In order to get jobs when they were adults, they needed a better education and so, when Charlotte was 14, she was sent away to a new school.

Charlotte's new school was much better than the one at Cowan Bridge. It was in a village called Roe Head, and was run by a kind, capable woman called Margaret Wooler, and her sisters. At first, Charlotte found it hard to fit in. She was awkward and shy, and so short-sighted that when she read a book, her nose almost touched the page. This made the other girls laugh. Most of them came from families that were richer than the Brontës, and Charlotte's worn, old-fashioned clothes made her stand out. Charlotte felt lonely and homesick, but before long she made two good friends. One was an energetic, independent girl called Mary Taylor, and the other was a quieter, gentle girl called Ellen Nussey.

Roe Head school

stories by candlelight

Charlotte knew that her school fees were expensive. She felt a duty to use her time at school as well as she could. She worked very hard at her lessons, and even spent breaktimes studying. In the evenings, she entertained the other girls by telling stories in the **dormitory**. One evening, Charlotte told a spooky story about a sleepwalker. It was so **vivid** and dramatic that a teacher had to be called to help calm down one of the terrified listeners. Charlotte felt guilty for frightening the girl too much, and decided not to tell spooky stories again.

After a year and a half, Charlotte left the school at Roe Head. She'd won prizes there for her excellent work, and now – aged 16 – she became a teacher at home for her sisters, Emily and Anne. She kept in touch with her school friends, Ellen and Mary, through letters and visits.

Charlotte also plunged back into writing about Angria, the imaginary land she and Branwell shared. Together – in partnership and in competition with one another – they developed new stories and characters. Charlotte often drew her characters, too. She loved drawing, and would spend hours copying pictures from books, or drawing portraits of people she knew.

one of Charlotte Brontë's paintings

Branwell, meanwhile, had decided he wanted to become a professional artist. He was taking lessons with a portrait painter, though the lessons were so expensive that Patrick Brontë could barely afford them.

# *Family portrait*

Around this time, Branwell painted a portrait of himself and his sisters. For some reason, he didn't like the figure of himself, so he painted it out. Many years later, the picture was found folded up on top of a cupboard. Now it hangs in the National Portrait Gallery in London. It's one of the most popular portraits with visitors – and you can still see the fold marks.

# Becoming a teacher

Charlotte would have loved to train as a painter like Branwell, but their father couldn't pay for them both to have lessons. Branwell's career plans were considered more important than Charlotte's, because he was a boy. Charlotte still needed to earn a living, though. So in 1835, when she was 19, she returned to her old school at Roe Head – this time as a teacher.

Charlotte's sister, Emily, accompanied her to Roe Head as a pupil. However, Emily was terribly unhappy at the school. She wasn't interested in making friends. She desperately missed the freedom of walking on the windswept moors at home in Haworth. She was desperate to be able to write about her imaginary land of Gondal too, and the school routine gave her no time. Soon, Emily was so homesick that she became ill. She left the school after three months, and the youngest Brontë sister, Anne, took her place.

Emily Brontë

Charlotte was very homesick too, but she had a strong sense of duty. She stayed at Roe Head and worked very hard as a teacher, though she didn't enjoy it. Secretly, she disliked her pupils, and felt impatient with them. She found it a huge strain to hide these feelings. As she became more miserable, her imaginary world was her only comfort. She longed to have time to write. Sometimes her imagination was so vivid that she saw people from Angria standing in the schoolroom.

Anne Brontë

Charlotte still dreamt of having her writing published one day. She wasn't alone: Branwell had been sending his poems to newspapers and magazines, hoping they'd be printed, but without success. When Charlotte went home for the Christmas holidays in 1836, she and Branwell each decided to write a letter to a famous author and ask for advice. Branwell wrote to the poet William Wordsworth, but he didn't reply.
Charlotte sent some of her work to Robert Southey, another famous poet. Southey did reply: he said that writing couldn't and shouldn't be the business of a woman's life. He told Charlotte that her real duties were to be a wife and mother.

Robert Southey

It wasn't long before Charlotte received two proposals of marriage from young clergymen – one of them was her friend Ellen's brother. She refused them both. She didn't want to marry a man she didn't love, even though marriage would have meant she could give up teaching.

By now all the Brontë children needed to earn their living, but it was a struggle. Branwell set himself up as a portrait painter in Bradford, but he didn't make enough money, and soon he came home again. When Emily was 20, she got a job as a schoolteacher. She had to work longer hours than Charlotte – from six in the morning until 11 at night. She was so miserable that she became ill again, and gave it up after less than a year.

Charlotte managed more than three years of teaching at the Roe Head school before she too gave up her job and came back to Haworth. Soon afterwards, her youngest sister Anne, who was now 19, found a job as a **governess**, and went to live with her employers at a large house about 30 kilometres from home.

For a while, the rest of the Brontë siblings lived together at the parsonage, along with their father and Aunt Branwell. Charlotte kept the house clean, while Emily cooked the food. Branwell – being male – wasn't expected to help around the house. The rest of the time they spent writing. Charlotte was beginning to explore new types of writing, using her own life experience in her stories as well as the fantasies from Angria. In the past, her writing had been closely connected to Branwell's. Now she was becoming more independent, and – as she practised more and more – her skills as a writer were growing.

Stonegappe

However, Charlotte couldn't stay at home, writing, forever. She knew she had to find a paid job. Inspired by Anne, she took a temporary post as a governess, living with a family called the Sidgwicks at a grand house called Stonegappe.

Charlotte soon found that she disliked being a governess even more than being a schoolteacher. Governesses weren't treated as the equals of the families that employed them, but as servants. Charlotte was expected to spend her evenings doing household sewing, sitting alone in the schoolroom. When guests visited the house, she was made to feel invisible. Since she was the daughter of a gentleman, Charlotte felt this was a **humiliation**. The children she was in charge of were badly behaved, too, and she was expected to wipe their noses and tie their shoelaces as well as teach them lessons – this, she hated.

a wealthy Victorian family and their governess

Charlotte was glad to leave the Sidgwicks when their regular governess returned. Later, she spent a few months as a governess with another family, the Whites, but she was unhappy there too and soon came home again.

All through her years at Roe Head and as a governess, Charlotte had kept in touch with her old friends from the school at Cowan Bridge, Mary Taylor and Ellen Nussey. Now Mary was travelling around Europe with her brother. She wrote letters to Charlotte describing the wonderful buildings and art she'd seen. Reading Mary's letters, Charlotte longed to spread her wings – to travel, to experience new places, to learn about art and culture. A plan began to form in her mind.

Mary Taylor in later life

Ellen Nussey in later life

For some time, Charlotte and her sisters, Emily and Anne, had been discussing the idea of opening their own school. They needed paid work, and if they had their own school, they would at least be in charge of their own lives, and would have one another's company. Now, inspired by Mary's letters, Charlotte persuaded her father and aunt that she and Emily first needed to go abroad to study. The extra skills they gained from this would help them attract more pupils when they set up their school.

Charlotte was determined and she argued well; her father and Aunt Branwell agreed. Charlotte found a good school in Brussels, Belgium, and in February 1842 – when she was 25 years old – she and Emily set out from Haworth. Their father accompanied them, since it was considered unsuitable for women to travel alone.

First, they went by train to London, which took 11 hours. Charlotte and Emily had never seen London before. They spent three days there, visiting places like the British Museum, the National Gallery, Westminster Abbey and St Paul's Cathedral, and Charlotte drank in every new sight eagerly.

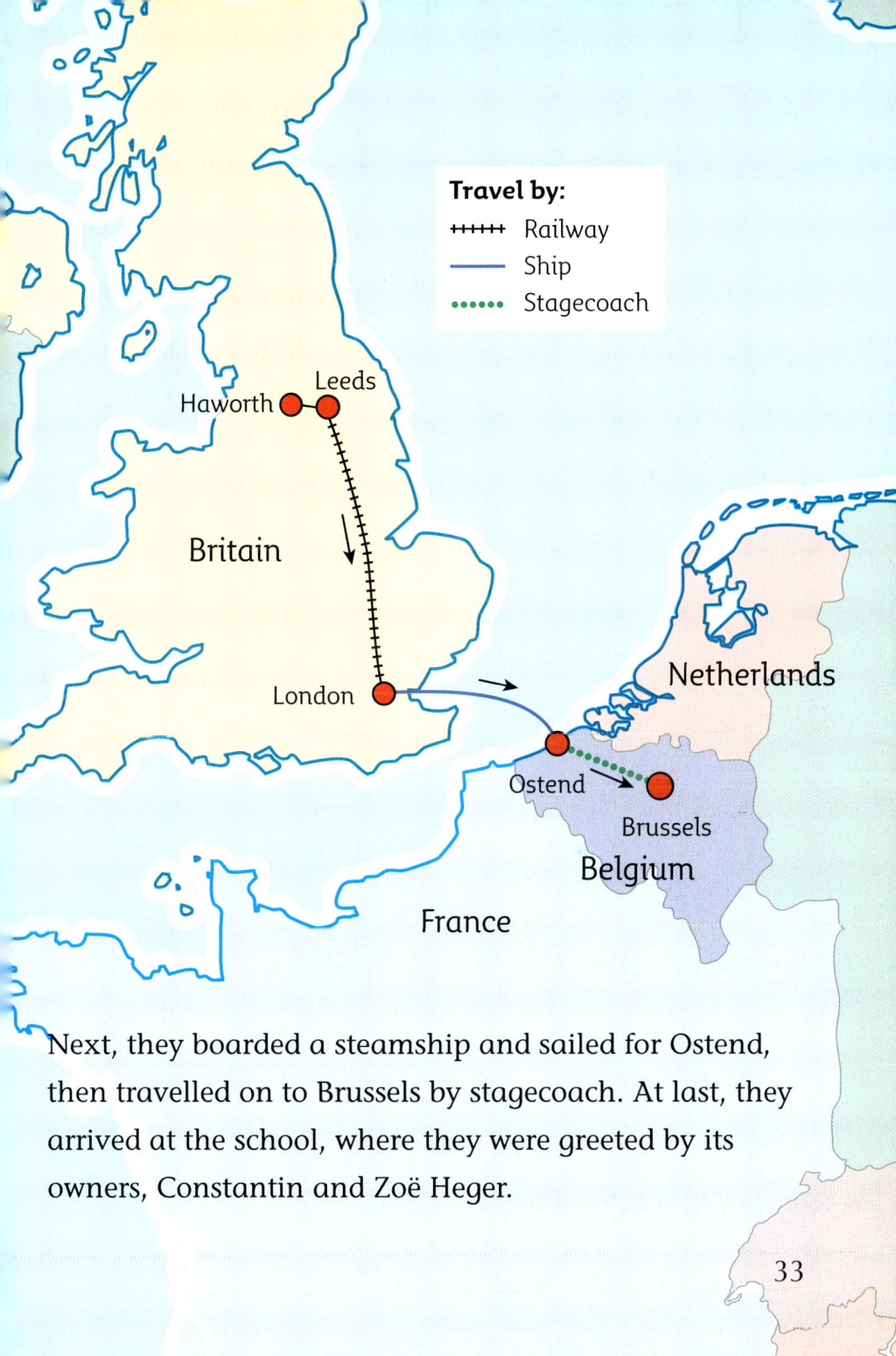

Next, they boarded a steamship and sailed for Ostend, then travelled on to Brussels by stagecoach. At last, they arrived at the school, where they were greeted by its owners, Constantin and Zoë Heger.

# Brussels

Charlotte and Emily were by far the oldest pupils at the Hegers' school, and they didn't try to make any friends. Instead, they concentrated on work. All the lessons were taught in French, which was especially difficult for Emily, who knew less French than Charlotte. Even so, they both made remarkable progress. It was strange for Charlotte to be a pupil once more, after teaching for so long, but she loved the chance to learn. Her favourite teacher was Monsieur Heger himself, who taught French literature. He was a **charismatic**, quick-tempered man, and an inspiring and demanding teacher.

Monsieur Heger in later life

Royal Galleries of Saint-Hubert in Brussels

Monsieur Heger quickly realised that Charlotte and Emily were brilliant writers, but he wanted them to improve still further. He was ruthlessly critical, especially of Charlotte's work, making her question every word she wrote. Sometimes he made her cry, but Charlotte recognised that Heger's method – by which she had to study great writers and copy their style – was transforming her own writing. She loved his fierce intelligence, his commitment to the work and his encouragement of her talent, and soon she became devoted to him.

After eight months in Brussels, Charlotte and Emily received the sad news that Aunt Branwell had died. They travelled home, though they arrived too late for the funeral. Emily was happy to stay, taking up her role as housekeeper at Haworth once more. She could walk each day on her beloved moors, and fit her writing and reading around her household duties. Sometimes, she'd prop open a German book on the kitchen table while she was kneading bread. Charlotte, however, wanted to return to Brussels, where she'd now started teaching.

Back in Brussels without Emily, Charlotte was lonely. Since she was a teacher instead of a pupil, she no longer had lessons with Monsieur Heger, though she sometimes still wrote essays for him to mark, and he gave her books to read. As so often before, Charlotte didn't enjoy her teaching, and her hero-worship of Monsieur Heger made life uncomfortable – she began to think that Madame Heger didn't like her. At last she decided to leave.

When she returned to Haworth, Charlotte found that – despite her Brussels education – she couldn't get enough pupils to open a school with her sisters.

Charlotte felt very low, and missed Monsieur Heger desperately. She longed for a life of travel and action, but couldn't see how to achieve it. She longed to be a writer, but believed that – as a woman – she could only be a teacher. Her life felt like a failure.

the Brontës' advertisement for their school

### The Misses Bronte's Establishment
FOR
**THE BOARD AND EDUCATION**
OF A LIMITED NUMBER OF
**YOUNG LADIES,**
## THE PARSONAGE, HAWORTH,
**NEAR BRADFORD.**

*Terms.*

| | £. | s. | d. |
|---|---|---|---|
| BOARD AND EDUCATION, including Writing, Arithmetic, History, Grammar, Geography, and Needle Work, per Annum, .. | 35 | 0 | 0 |
| French, .. German, .. Latin .. } each per Quarter, | 1 | 1 | 0 |
| Music, .. Drawing, .. } each per Quarter, | 1 | 1 | 0 |
| Use of Piano Forte, per Quarter, .. | 0 | 5 | 0 |
| Washing, per Quarter, .. | 0 | 15 | 0 |

Each Young Lady to be provided with One Pair of Sheets, Pillow Cases, Four Towels, a Dessert and Tea-spoon.

A Quarter's Notice, or a Quarter's Board, is required previous to the Removal of a Pupil.

# A chance discovery

By the summer of 1845, the Brontë siblings were all back at home. Anne had been working as a governess, but had finally given up her job after much unhappiness. Branwell – who was talented, but **rash** and careless – had been sacked from three different jobs. He'd succeeded in getting published, however: almost 20 of his poems had been printed in the newspapers over the last four years. He now began to write a novel, which he hoped would earn more money than poetry.

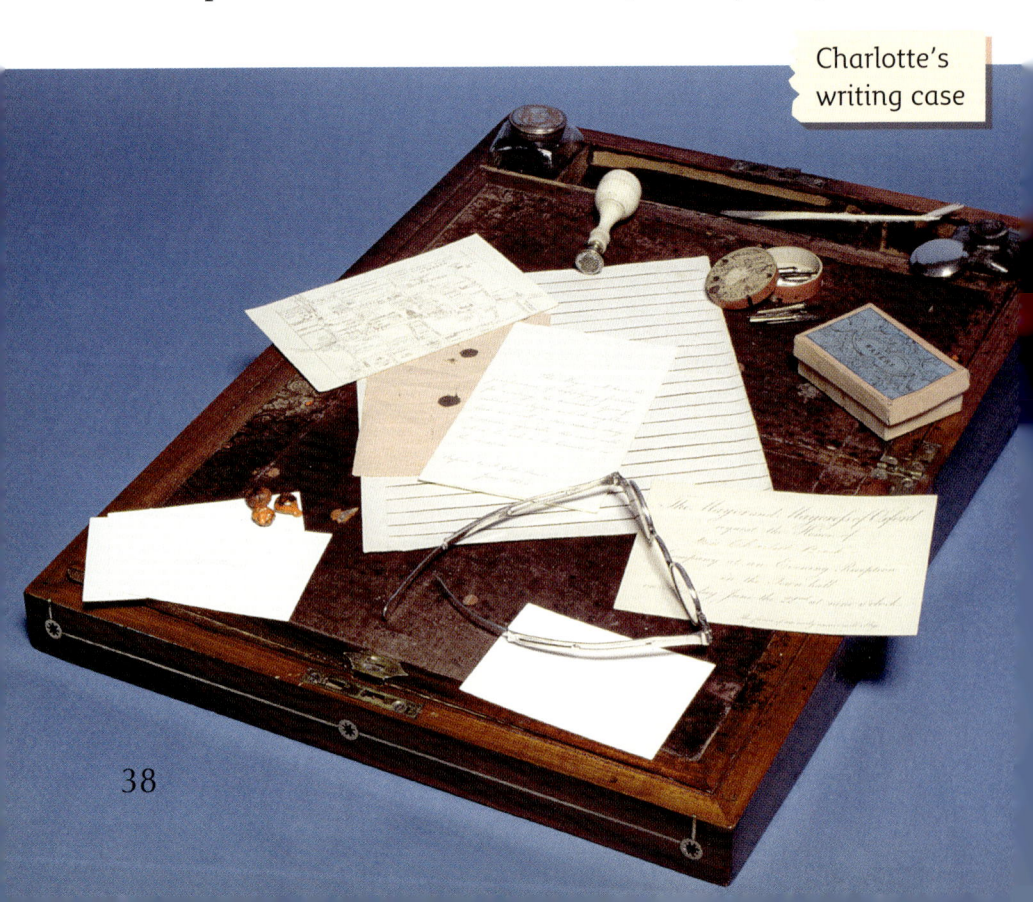

Charlotte's writing case

Then, one day in the autumn of 1845, Charlotte found a notebook of Emily's poems. For many years, Emily and Anne had shared their writing with one another, but not with Charlotte or Branwell. Now, reading Emily's poems, Charlotte was very impressed. Emily was furious when she found out, but Charlotte was inspired. The sisters needed to earn money, and Charlotte's friend, Mary Taylor, often said that women shouldn't rely on men, as everyone expected – they should act for themselves. So Charlotte formed a daring plan: to get the poems published. It took days to persuade Emily, but at last she agreed. Together with Anne, they made a collection of poems by all three sisters. However, they decided to keep their identities secret. In particular, they didn't want anyone to know that the poems were written by women.

Even though there was now a woman – Queen Victoria – on the British throne, women were still believed to be inferior to men. As Robert Southey had told Charlotte, writing wasn't considered a woman's business.
Critics didn't take women's writing seriously.
They thought that if women insisted on writing, they should only write about certain "ladylike" topics. However, the Brontë sisters wanted their work to be taken as seriously as any man's. So they decided to use **pseudonyms**. The sisters didn't want to choose men's names because that felt to them like telling a lie. Instead, they chose names that were neither male nor female. Each name used their real initials: Charlotte was Currer Bell, Emily was Ellis Bell and Anne was Acton Bell.

Without telling Branwell or their father, Charlotte wrote letters to several publishers. At last she found a small publishing company in London that was willing to accept the poetry collection – but only if the "Bells" paid for publication themselves. Charlotte and her sisters agreed, though it must have been difficult for them to afford it. They were delighted when at last the finished books arrived – they'd realised their childhood dream of becoming published authors! But still they didn't tell anyone about it.

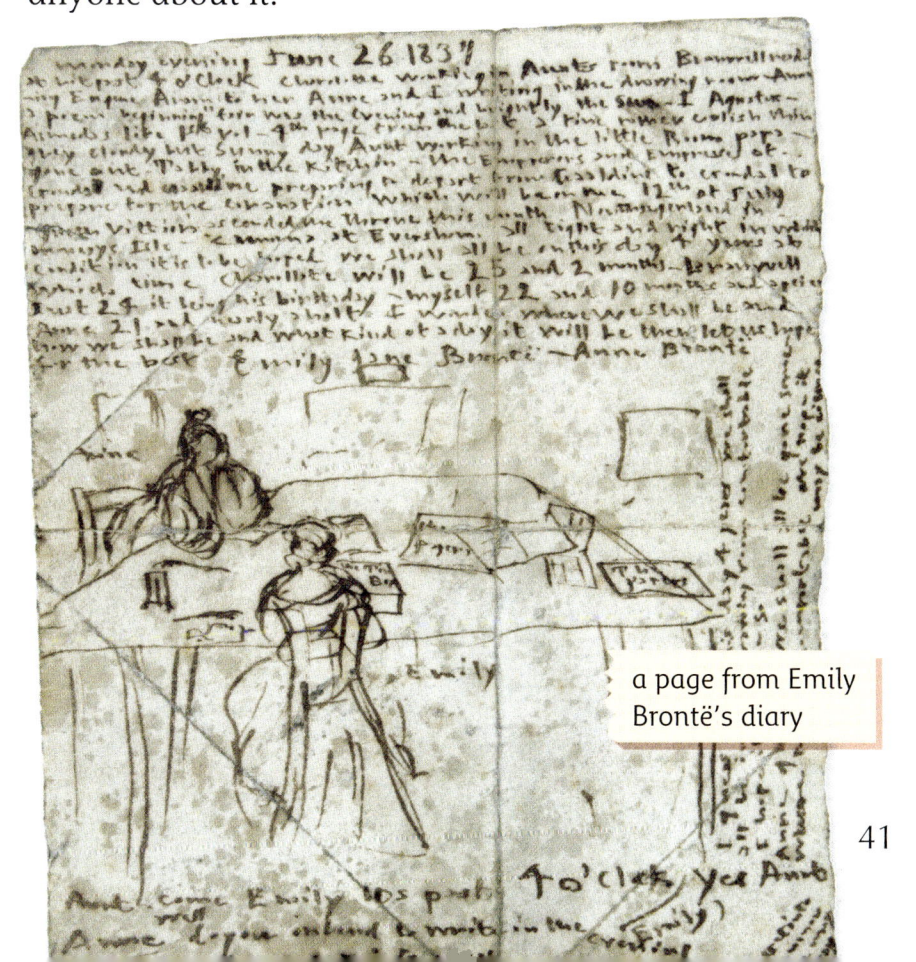

a page from Emily Brontë's diary

During its first year in print, the poetry collection only sold two copies, but Charlotte wasn't **discouraged**. Pursuing her own projects – which Victorians thought, for a woman, was "selfish" – made Charlotte happy. Now, she and her sisters began writing novels. Like Branwell, they thought novels were more likely to earn them some money. Branwell had given up his novel halfway through, but Charlotte, Emily and Anne were more determined. They supported one another in their writing. Sometimes they read pages aloud and asked each other's opinion. In the evenings, they walked round and round the dining table, secretly discussing their stories.

By July 1846, all three novels were finished. Charlotte's was called *The Professor*, and was inspired by Monsieur Heger. Emily's was called *Wuthering Heights*, and it was closely connected to her writing about Gondal. Anne's novel was called *Agnes Grey* – it was about a governess, and it drew on Anne's own experience.

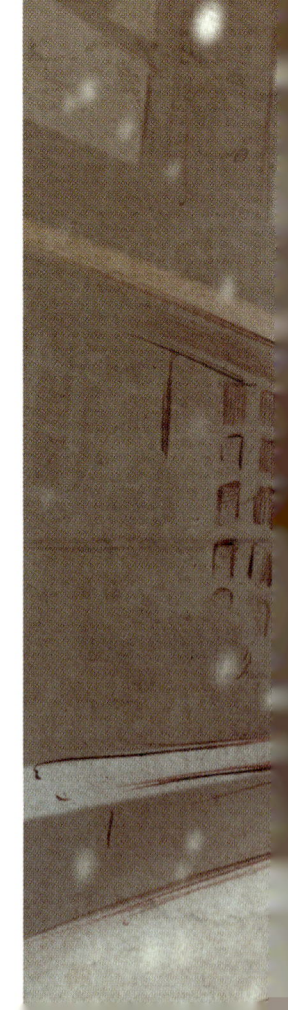

Charlotte wrapped the three novels in a brown paper parcel and sent them off to a London publisher.
The publisher rejected them and sent them back.
So Charlotte crossed out the address of the first publisher, and wrote on the parcel a different publisher's address. In this way, the parcel went back and forth between Haworth and London for a whole year. Publisher after publisher rejected the novels.

Meanwhile, Charlotte and her sisters had to spend more and more time looking after their father, Patrick. He was going blind and needed an operation to restore his sight. Charlotte went with him to Manchester, where there was a specialist eye hospital. Patrick had the operation without **anaesthetic**, and stayed in Manchester for a month to recover. During this time with her father, Charlotte began to write a new novel: *Jane Eyre*.

# Jane Eyre

*Jane Eyre* is the story of a young orphan girl. She lives at first with her aunt and cousins, who all treat her cruelly. Then she is sent away to a harsh school – very like Charlotte's own school at Cowan Bridge. The character of Jane's best friend, who dies, is based on Charlotte's eldest sister, Maria. When Jane is old enough to work, she becomes a governess (as Charlotte did), working for a rich man called Mr Rochester. Mr Rochester's grand house is full of secrets. Jane hears strange noises in the attic, and soon mysterious things begin to happen. The story is dramatic and exciting, with vivid descriptions of people and places. Jane is a brave and passionate character, and she tells people what she thinks of them, even if they are the people – like her aunt or Mr Rochester – whom she's supposed to obey. The story is told through Jane's eyes, as if she's speaking directly to the reader. This makes the novel even more gripping.

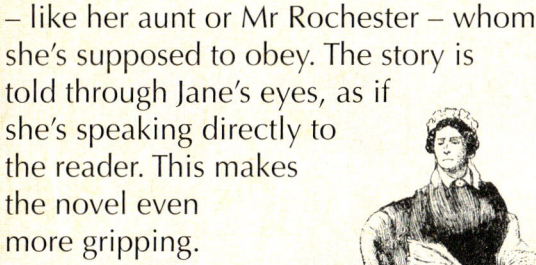

This illustration shows the young Jane Eyre with her aunt and the headmaster from her school.

While Charlotte was working on *Jane Eyre*, the parcel of three novels by Currer, Ellis and Acton Bell was still looking for a home. At last, a publisher accepted Emily and Anne's books – *Wuthering Heights* and *Agnes Grey* – but only if the authors paid for publication themselves. Reluctantly, Emily and Anne agreed. Charlotte refused to give up. She carried on sending her book – *The Professor* – to other publishers. She was determined not to pay for publication.

The seventh publisher Charlotte tried was called Smith, Elder, & Co. They didn't think *The Professor* would sell, but they believed this author showed promise. So they wrote to "Currer Bell", asking if "he" had another novel to show them. Quickly, Charlotte finished *Jane Eyre* and sent it off.

George Smith, owner of Smith, Elder, & Co.

George Smith, the owner of the company, began to read *Jane Eyre* one Sunday morning. He couldn't put it down; he cancelled all his appointments and even ate dinner at his desk while he read. The next day he offered Currer Bell £100 for the right to publish the novel. This was more than half the sum Charlotte's father earned in a year, and five times her own salary as a governess. Though she still had money worries, it was a good start, and she was delighted.

the offices of Smith, Elder, & Co.

# Publication

Six weeks later, in October 1847, *Jane Eyre* was published. No one had read anything like it before, and it quickly became a bestseller. Charlotte's publishers sent a copy to one of her favourite writers, William Makepeace Thackeray, the author of a famous novel called *Vanity Fair*. Thackeray liked it very much, and said some parts made him cry. This praise from her hero meant a great deal to Charlotte.

Readers were especially gripped by the character of Jane. She battled against injustice and said that women and men were equal. It was astonishing for an ordinary woman to argue like this, and people wondered who'd created her.

William Makepeace Thackeray

The publishers had added a subtitle – An **Autobiography** – which made people suspect that Currer Bell was a woman. To some people this made the book even more shocking. Women in Victorian times weren't supposed to be like Jane Eyre, with her independent mind and strong feelings. Many critics praised the book for being powerful, clever and original, but some said it was "**immoral**" and "unfeminine".

Two months after *Jane Eyre* was published, Emily's *Wuthering Heights* and Anne's *Agnes Grey* appeared in print. Critics took little notice of *Agnes Grey*, but *Wuthering Heights* was the subject of much public discussion.

Thackeray with a group of his writer friends in the 1830s

Like *Jane Eyre*, *Wuthering Heights* is today considered a masterpiece. The story is set on Emily's beloved moorland, and centres on the relationship between Catherine – the daughter of a gentleman – and Heathcliff, a wild homeless boy who is adopted by Catherine's father. Victorian readers found it **spellbinding**, but it challenged their ideas about religion, social class and relations between men and women, and some characters were cruel and violent. One critic said that in terms of imaginative power it was "one of the greatest novels in the language", but he also said it was "coarse". Soon other critics began to say that there was unrespectable behaviour in all of the Bells' books.

the Yorkshire moors

Charlotte and her sisters were upset by the criticisms, but they were also encouraged by the praise. The success of *Jane Eyre* gave them hope that they could make a living from writing. Emily and Anne began work on new novels. Although they kept their own books a secret, they encouraged Charlotte to tell their father about the success of *Jane Eyre*. Charlotte hesitated. She wasn't sure what Patrick would say, and she enjoyed the freedom of writing **anonymously**. Then one day, she overheard the postman asking Patrick where Currer Bell lived. Patrick said there was no one of that name in the parish. This made up Charlotte's mind. She told her father that she was Currer Bell and that *Jane Eyre* was her own book. To her relief, Patrick wasn't angry. Over time, he became very proud of her success.

Though Charlotte's father now knew her secret, she didn't tell anyone else – not even the servants in the parsonage, or her close friend Ellen. Her publishers weren't sure of her true identity either. Then, in June 1848, Anne's publisher – whose name was Thomas Newby – brought out her second novel, *The Tenant of Wildfell Hall*. Newby wanted to profit from *Jane Eyre*'s success, so he claimed that this novel was by the same author as *Jane Eyre*, and that all three Bells were really one person.

When Charlotte's publisher, George Smith, heard this he was alarmed and angry, and he wrote to Currer Bell demanding an explanation. As soon as Smith's letter arrived, Charlotte wanted to set off for London with Emily and Anne, to show him the truth. Emily refused to go – she was determined to remain anonymous. Charlotte argued with her all day, but it was no use. In the late afternoon, Charlotte and Anne set off without Emily. They walked four miles through a thunderstorm to reach the station, and then took the night train to London.

Charlotte and Anne arrived in London at eight o'clock in the morning. They went to the Chapter Coffee House near St Paul's Cathedral, where Charlotte, Emily and Patrick had stayed before setting off for Brussels six years before. There, they washed and had breakfast, then set out to find the offices of Smith, Elder, & Co.

Coffee houses were popular places for men to meet their friends. Overnight guests could pay to stay in upstairs rooms.

At the front of the publisher's offices was a busy bookshop. Stepping inside, Charlotte asked one of the staff if she could see Mr Smith. George Smith was busy in a back room and didn't want to be disturbed, but Charlotte insisted. He came out and saw two small, pale women waiting. One of them – Charlotte – put a letter into his hand; it was his own letter, addressed to Currer Bell. Smith asked where she'd got it. Charlotte was amused at his puzzlement, and told him she was Miss Brontë. Smith had been instructed to send some of Currer Bell's post to a "Miss Brontë", so he knew the name. Privately, he'd suspected that Miss Brontë and Currer Bell were the same person – now he knew for sure.

George Smith was delighted by Charlotte and Anne's visit, and wanted to introduce them to London society. The newspapers were full of rumours about the Bell "brothers", and he knew people would be astonished to discover their true identity. Charlotte and Anne said no – they hated the idea of being stared at and talked about. They wanted to maintain their disguise.

George Smith entertained Charlotte and Anne, taking them to dinners and to the opera, but he couldn't tell anyone they were famous authors. Charlotte knew that the rich men and women she met looked down on her, thinking she was a **quaint**, unfashionable countrywoman. The same kind of people had ignored her when she was a governess. She was amused to think how differently they would have acted if they'd known she was the author of *Jane Eyre*.

Meanwhile Anne's novel *The Tenant of Wildfell Hall* was selling very well, and rumours were flying in Yorkshire about who the Bells might really be. Readers who knew Charlotte's old school at Cowan Bridge had recognised her depiction of it in *Jane Eyre*, complete with a headmaster very like the real one. But writing secretly meant the Brontë sisters could write freely – just as it had when they were children. With her identity still undisclosed, Charlotte began a new novel. However, events at home soon made her stop writing.

Branwell was very ill. Heartbroken after a failed relationship, he'd been living a wild lifestyle for several years, and at last his health had broken down. Now, on top of this, he'd developed tuberculosis. Two and a half months after Charlotte and Anne's return from London, he died at home in Haworth, at the age of 31.

Branwell drew this **caricature** of himself in 1847. He's in bed, waiting to die.

# Sorrowful times

Charlotte's grief was intense – but worse was yet to come. A month after Branwell's death, Charlotte began to worry about her sisters' health. Soon it became clear that they too had tuberculosis. Emily died in December 1848, two months after Branwell, and Anne died the following May.

Charlotte was devastated. She'd lost all her remaining siblings in less than a year. Only she and her grief-stricken father were left at Haworth, and the parsonage felt horribly empty. In the evenings, when Patrick had retired to bed, Charlotte would walk round and round the dining room, just as she'd done with her sisters when they discussed their writing. Now, though, Charlotte walked alone.

the dining room at Haworth

Ever since childhood, writing had been something Charlotte had done alongside Branwell, Emily and Anne. They'd discussed their plots and characters together, argued and laughed over their imaginary worlds, read aloud their half-finished chapters, and helped each other to improve their stories and writing styles. All that companionship had now vanished, and Charlotte said her brain felt like a "silent workshop". Still, she knew she had to work. Writing, she told a friend, was her "best companion". So she began to work again on the novel she'd been writing before Branwell died.

Charlotte's new novel was called *Shirley*, and it told the story of two women, one of whom – Shirley Keeldar – was partly based on Emily. The novel was set in Yorkshire in the years just before Charlotte's birth, when there were riots because of widespread poverty and the new technology that was threatening workers' livelihoods. Although Charlotte set *Shirley* in the past, the novel was a commentary on her own time, too: the 1840s was also a period of protest and desperate poverty. Conditions were so hard for the poor that the decade has since been called "The Hungry Forties".

*Shirley* wasn't just about poverty and industry – it was also about the position of women in society. It communicated Charlotte's passionate belief in women's right to work, and it challenged Victorian views about women's nature and education.

*Shirley* was published in October 1849 – a year after Branwell's death. Reviewers gave it a mixture of praise and criticism, but Charlotte felt that London critics didn't understand life in the north; her readers in Yorkshire and Lancashire understood her work much better.

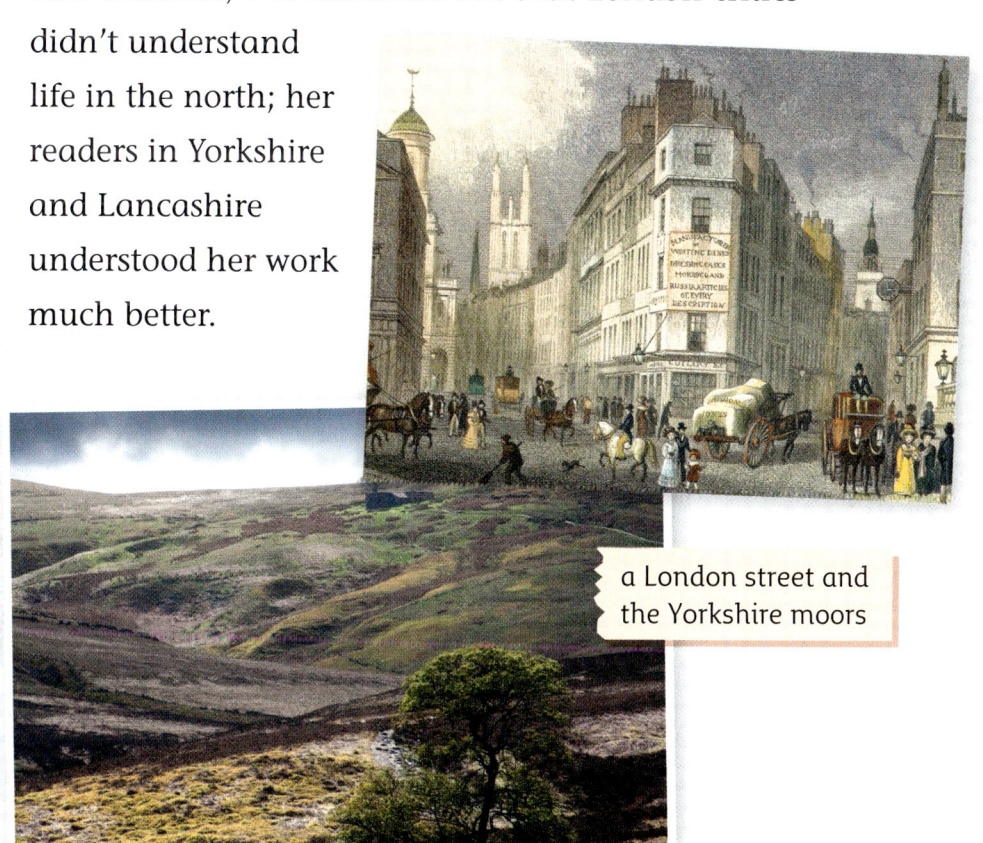

a London street and the Yorkshire moors

*Shirley* included a scene in which one of the characters is very seriously ill and, in writing it, Charlotte drew on her experience of looking after her dying siblings. After reading it, another writer – Elizabeth Gaskell – wrote to Currer Bell to say how moved she was.

Elizabeth Gaskell

Three of Mrs Gaskell's own children had died, and she recognised that the author of *Shirley* wrote from painful personal experience.

Mrs Gaskell was well known for her short stories, and had had her first novel, *Mary Barton*, published the year before *Shirley* came out. She'd published *Mary Barton* anonymously, but her identity had soon been revealed. Now Charlotte's anonymity was also fading.

A parcel from her publishers was mysteriously opened on its journey between London and Haworth – by someone, Charlotte guessed, who wanted to discover the identity of Currer Bell. In towns and cities across Yorkshire, gossip now linked Bell's books to Miss Brontë of Haworth.

Charlotte was annoyed and dismayed. She hated being the focus of people's curiosity, and she knew that readers would judge the characters in her books as portraits of herself and people she knew. But as news of her authorship spread, she found that people in Haworth were very proud of her. She especially valued the tributes she received from ordinary working people who'd read her books.

# A taste of fame

The fact that Haworth was proud of Charlotte pleased her father, Patrick – and Charlotte was glad about this. Neither of them liked it, however, when strangers began turning up at the parsonage, wanting to meet Currer Bell. Charlotte didn't like visits from "curiosity-hunters", as she called them, even though life at the parsonage was lonely. To combat the loneliness, Charlotte's publisher George Smith several times invited her to London. There, Charlotte visited places that interested her, such as London Zoo, the Great Exhibition at Hyde Park, and the Foundling Hospital for orphans. She also found that, now her identity as an author was known, clever, **literary** people wanted to spend time with her.

London Zoo

The Great Exhibition was held in a building called the Crystal Palace.

In London, most people's first impression of Charlotte was that she was small, timid and shy. She was nervous of parties filled with people she didn't know, and sometimes she trembled. However, people also noticed her bright, piercing gaze, and when a discussion began on a topic that interested her, Charlotte's shyness fell away: she gave her views so bluntly that she sometimes stunned dinner parties into silence. She wasn't even afraid of telling her hero Thackeray what his faults as a writer were – in particular that his stories were unfair to women. And Charlotte never forgot her own experience before she'd become famous: at one party at Thackeray's house, she spent most of the evening talking with the family's governess, because she knew that governesses were usually ignored.

On one visit to London, George Smith persuaded Charlotte to have her portrait painted by the artist George Richmond. Charlotte considered herself ugly, and found sitting for Richmond agonising. When she saw the finished portrait, she wept and said it looked like Anne. But her father was delighted, and said the portrait showed Charlotte's genius. He hung it in the parsonage.

In 1850, Smith, Elder, & Co. suggested publishing new editions of Emily and Anne's novels, *Wuthering Heights* and *Agnes Grey*. Charlotte agreed, and decided to make a new collection of her sisters' poetry, too. Before submitting the poems for publication, however, she made quite a few changes. Some changes removed references to the imaginary world of Gondal, and it's likely that Emily and Anne would have approved of these. But the other changes Charlotte made would probably have infuriated them. Charlotte was their elder sister, and was keen to protect their reputation, but it's hard to know why she tried to "improve" their work. She also prevented Anne's second novel, *The Tenant of Wildfell Hall*, from being republished.

*The Tenant of Wildfell Hall* is about a woman who leaves her cruel husband, taking her young son with her. This was deeply shocking to Victorian society, because married women then couldn't divorce their husbands, or own property, or have rights over their children. Although Charlotte didn't like the story, today it's considered a brilliant and important novel.

The process of going through Emily and Anne's papers had been hugely painful for Charlotte. She missed her sisters terribly. When she walked on the moors, every beautiful view, every plant, flower and creature she saw reminded her of their absence. Although trips to London were a cheering distraction, at home Charlotte felt very low. She'd turned down a marriage proposal from one of the managers at her publishers, and – with her father's health declining – she saw a lonely future ahead of her. What's more, she was finding it hard to write. Charlotte was anxious not to disappoint her publishers and her father, but now that Emily and Anne were no longer writing alongside her, and now that she felt **scrutinised** by public opinion, writing was harder than ever.

This picture is from a modern film of *Jane Eyre*.

However, Charlotte *did* write, even though the process was slower and more painful than ever before. The result was a novel called *Villette*, which was published in January 1853.

## *Villette*

*Villette* is the story of Lucy Snowe, an intelligent, plain and reserved woman who teaches at a girls' school in Villette, a fictional city based on Brussels. The novel features several characters inspired by people Charlotte knew, including Monsieur Heger and George Smith. It's a fierce, powerful story, and very cleverly written; Lucy is an unreliable narrator who keeps secrets from the reader, and the story is as much about Lucy's thoughts and emotions as it is about events. Through *Villette*, Charlotte expressed her anger at the way women in her time were trapped by social rules.

# Changes at home

Charlotte was disappointed that her publishers only paid her £500 for *Villette*, when they'd paid Mrs Gaskell £2,000 for her latest novel. She still had money worries, because Haworth parsonage belonged to the Church, so she'd have to find a new home when her father died. But she was cheered by the reviews of *Villette*, which were more consistently positive than for her previous books.

By the time *Villette* was published, dramatic events had occurred in Charlotte's home life. One evening in December 1852, she was sitting alone in the dining room when there was a knock on the door. It was Patrick Brontë's **curate**, Arthur Bell Nicholls. Charlotte was surprised to see that he was trembling with emotion; when he managed to speak, he asked her to marry him. Charlotte had known Arthur for seven years, she liked and respected him and she was moved now by his strength of feeling. But when she told her father about Arthur's proposal, Patrick flew into such a rage that Charlotte feared for his health. She promised to turn the proposal down.

Patrick was so angry that he refused to speak to Arthur. He thought it would be **degrading** for Charlotte to marry Arthur, because he was too poor. He was also furious that Arthur hadn't asked his permission before proposing. Charlotte didn't agree with Patrick's views. She felt sorry for Arthur, and upset at the way her father was treating him.

Arthur Bell Nicholls

Arthur gave up his job, and left Haworth. Soon, however, he began to write letters to Charlotte and, without telling her father, she wrote letters in return. Slowly, Charlotte's affection for Arthur grew. She told Patrick he'd been unfair to Arthur and reassured him that, even if she got married, she would stay at the parsonage to look after him. Eventually, she persuaded Patrick to agree to the marriage, and the wedding took place in June 1854.

Charlotte and Arthur shared the same sense of humour, and their marriage was very happy. After the wedding, Patrick and Arthur got on well again, too. Arthur took over Patrick's parish duties, and Charlotte spent all her time helping him. Before her marriage she'd been working on a new novel – *Emma* – but now she didn't have time to write.

Charlotte Brontë's wedding bonnet and veil

Six months after marrying Arthur, in January 1855, Charlotte fell ill. She couldn't stop being sick, and suspected she might be pregnant. It's now thought that Charlotte had *hyperemesis gravidarum*, a condition that causes excessive vomiting during pregnancy. Today, this can be successfully treated, but in Charlotte's time there was nothing the doctors could do. As she became weaker and weaker, Arthur nursed her devotedly. Charlotte told him she didn't think God would separate them, as they'd been so happy – and together such a short time. However, on 31 March 1855, Charlotte died. She was 38 years old.

# Legacy

After Charlotte's death, Arthur stayed on in Haworth and looked after Patrick until he died, six years later. Arthur remained devoted to Charlotte's memory and when, after Patrick's death, he had to move away, he carefully kept a wealth of manuscripts, pictures, clothes and other personal items. He guarded Charlotte's privacy fiercely, and destroyed some items that he felt were too private. Nevertheless, it's in large part thanks to Arthur that now Haworth parsonage – which has become a museum – is once again full of manuscripts and objects made or used by the Brontë family.

Haworth parsonage today

Today, more than 150 years after her death, Charlotte Brontë is considered not only one of the greatest English novelists, but also a ground-breaking and innovative pioneer for her portrayal of women's lives. Her books – and those of her sisters – are read and studied all over the world. Of Charlotte's three novels, *Jane Eyre* is still the most well-known – as it was in her lifetime. Along with Emily's novel *Wuthering Heights*, *Jane Eyre* has been one of the most popular Victorian novels with 20th- and 21st-century writers and filmmakers, who've adapted it many times for the stage and screen.

As a result of this huge popularity, more than 70,000 people travel to Haworth each year, to walk in the footsteps of Charlotte and her sisters on the moorland they loved, and to visit the parsonage where their wonderful books were written.

This picture is from a modern film of *Jane Eyre*.

# Glossary

| | |
|---|---|
| **anaesthetic** | substance that blocks pain |
| **anonymously** | without revealing the person's identity |
| **autobiography** | true story of a person's life, written by himself/herself |
| **caricature** | a picture or description exaggerating a situation |
| **charismatic** | having a fascinating charm |
| **clergyman** | priest |
| **curate** | priest who is an assistant to a more senior priest |
| **degrading** | shaming; reducing someone to a lower rank |
| **discouraged** | lacking courage or hope |
| **dormitory** | large, shared sleeping room with many beds |
| **eccentric** | (of a person) of strange or unusual behaviour |
| **genii** | plural of genie (a magical creature or spirit) |
| **governess** | female teacher, employed in a private household |
| **humiliation** | something causing shame or embarrassment |
| **immoral** | against accepted rules of behaviour |
| **inferior** | not as valuable as |
| **inspired** | gave ideas or courage |
| **literary** | (of people) interested in the writing of books |
| **moorlands** | large open areas of unfarmed land |
| **parish** | church district |
| **parsonage** | a type of church house |
| **pioneering** | involving new ideas |
| **pseudonyms** | false names |
| **quaint** | strange or odd, especially in an old-fashioned way |
| **rash** | (of people) acting without thinking of the results |
| **scrutinised** | looked at very closely |
| **spellbinding** | holding the attention completely, as if by magic |
| **vivid** | clear, full of life, and detailed |

# Index

**Agnes Grey**  42, 46, 49, 67
**Angria**  18, 22, 25, 28
**Aunt Branwell (Elizabeth Branwell)**  7–8, 14, 28, 32, 36
**Bell, Acton**  40, 46
**Bell, Ellis**  40, 46
**Bell, Currer**  40, 46–47, 49, 51, 53, 55, 62–64
**Bell Nicholls, Arthur**  70–74
**Brontë, Anne**  4, 14–16, 18, 22, 24, 27, 29, 32, 38–40, 42, 46, 49, 51–59, 66–68
**Brontë, Branwell**  4, 14–16, 18, 22–24, 26–28, 38–39, 41–42, 57–59, 61
**Brontë, Elizabeth**  11, 13
**Brontë, Emily**  4, 11, 14–16, 18, 22, 24, 27–28, 32–36, 39–40, 42, 46, 49–51, 53–54, 58–60, 67–68, 75
**Brontë, Maria (mother)**  7
**Brontë, Maria**  8, 11, 13, 45
**Brontë, Rvd. Patrick**  4, 7, 10–11, 22, 44, 51, 54, 58, 64, 70–72, 74
**Brussels**  32–37, 54, 69
**Cowan Bridge**  11, 13, 20, 31, 45, 57
**Haworth**  5–6, 24, 27, 32, 36, 43, 57–58, 63–64, 70, 72, 74–75
**Heger, Constantin**  33–37, 42, 69

**Gaskell, Elizabeth**  62, 70
**Gondal**  18, 24, 42, 67
*Jane Eyre*  44–52, 56–57, 68, 75
**London**  23, 32, 41, 43, 53–55, 57, 61, 63–66, 68
**Newby, Thomas**  52
**Nussey, Ellen**  20 22, 26, 31, 52
*Professor, The*  42, 46
**Queen Victoria**  40
**Richmond, George**  66
**Roe Head**  20, 22, 24–25, 27, 31
*Shirley*  60–62
**Smith, Elder, & Co.**  46, 54, 67
**Smith, George**  47, 53, 55–56, 64, 66, 69
**Southey, Robert**  26, 40
**Taylor, Mary**  20, 22, 31–32, 39
*Tenant of Wildfell Hall, The*  52, 57, 67
**Thackeray, William Makepeace**  48–49, 65
**Thornton**  4
*Villette*  69–70
**Wooler, Margaret**  20
**Wordsworth, William**  26
*Wuthering Heights*  42, 46, 49–50, 67, 75
**Yorkshire**  4–5, 7, 50, 57, 60–61, 63

# The Brontës' world

home

family

school

imaginary worlds

travel

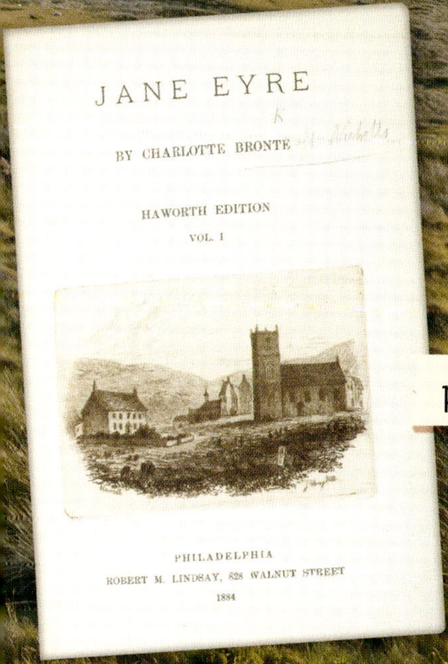

published books

79

# Ideas for reading

Written by Clare Dowdall, PhD
*Lecturer and Primary Literacy Consultant*

**Reading objectives:**
- ask questions to improve their understanding
- draw inferences and justify these with evidence
- retrieve, record and present information from non-fiction
- provide reasoned justifications for their views

**Spoken language objectives:**
- participate in discussions, presentations, performances, role play, improvisations and debates

**Curriculum links:** History – British history; Victorian England

**Resources:** A4 paper for minibook, pencils, ICT for research

## Build a context for reading

- Explain that you will be reading a biography. Explore what children know about biographies, discussing any that they have read.
- Look at the cover and read the blurb. Check whether anyone has heard of Charlotte Brontë, or her famous novel *Jane Eyre*. Ask children to suggest when she lived.
- Turn to the contents. Read them through and discuss how this biography is structured. Ask children which sections interest them the most and why.

## Understand and apply reading strategies

- Read pp2–3 together. Ask children what they know about Charlotte Brontë from this introduction and note their ideas on a whiteboard. As a group, separate their ideas into two groups: stated and inferred. Discuss how we can make inferences from information provided.
- Discuss women's lives in Victorian times. Look at the emboldened word *inferior*. Ask children to suggest a definition for this word, based on their reading. Check their ideas against the definition in the glossary.